Selling Essentials

Your First 90 Days In Selling

By Claude Whitacre

Copyright ©2016 Claude Whitacre
All Rights Reserved.
ISBN-10: 153720128X
ISBN-13: 978-1537201283

TABLE OF CONTENTS

Introduction ---------------------------------- Page 1
Who should read this book? -------------- Page 3
New In Sales? Read This ------------------ Page 9

Chapter 1
So.....What Is Selling...Really? ---------- Page 15

Chapter 2
What Is A Great Salesperson? ---------- Page 19

Chapter 3
How Your Sales Manager Can Make You Money. -------------------------------- Page 21

Chapter 4
Beginner Myths That New Salespeople Believe, And The Reality Behind Them. -- Page 23

Chapter 5
Essential Methods To Build A Foundation In Your Sales Career ------ Page 35

Chapter 6
The Fastest Way To See Sales Made. -- Page 41

Chapter 7
How To Overcome Your Fear Of Rejection. ----------------------------------- Page 45

Chapter 8
The Single Biggest Threat To Your Success, And How To Avoid It. --------- Page 49

Chapter 9
The Best Way To Build A Sales Career. -- Page 57

Chapter 10
The Best Tool A Company Can Give You To Guarantee Your Sales ---------- **Page 61**

Chapter 11
The Surest Way To Guarantee Steady Increases In Sales. ------------------------- **Page 67**

Chapter 12
The Single Best People To Sell To, When You Are Starting Out. ------------- **Page 71**

Chapter 13
What All Successful Salespeople Have In Common. ------------------------- **Page 77**

Chapter 14
The First Skill To Learn To Fill Your Pipeline With Buyers. --------------------- **Page 81**

Chapter 15
A Guaranteed Way To Get A Sale Right Now, And Win That Contest. --- **Page 85**

Chapter 16
The Key To Scheduling That Maximizes Sales. ---------------------------- **Page 89**

Chapter 17
Fast Start Methods That Will Jump Start Your Career. ------------------------ **Page 93**

Chapter 18
Salary Or Commission - Which Is Better? --------------------------------------- **Page 99**

Chapter 19
The Single Best Selling Secret To Send Your Sales Through The Roof. --------- **Page 103**

Chapter 20
This Technique Will Practically Guarantee A Sale And Keep The Prospect From Shopping. ----------------- **Page 111**

Chapter 21
Questions You Must Know The Answer To. ---------------------------------- **Page 113**

Chapter 22
The Biggest Secret Of The Sales Superstars...... Continuous Learning And Training ------------------------------- **Page 117**

About The Author -------------------------- **Page 121**

Recommended Reading -------------------- **Page 123**

Introduction.

The reason for my hesitation in writing this book was that it's so easy to talk about subjects that are a little advanced for a new salesperson. I also don't want to offer advice that may be slightly different than something coming from the company. There are many approaches to selling that all work.

If you have read anything else by me, or have heard me speak to a sales group, you have heard me say that what a salesperson does their first few weeks determines the direction they go with their company. Work habits are formed. A framework for teaching sales methods is established. The company culture is absorbed. The first month, is the most important month.

It's important for you to start off in the right direction, and not pick up bad habits that will derail your career.

Direction is destination.

"Whatever the new salesperson is like after the first couple of weeks, is pretty much what they will be like the rest of their time with your company. Habits are formed, work ethic is established, and the way they view you and the company is pretty well set."

– Claude Whitacre

Who should read this book?

If you are new in selling, where your income is determined by how much you sell, this book is for you. If you are the Sales Manager and have new salespeople working with you you'll also get a lot out of this book.

Here is who this book is *not* for.
This book is not for advanced salespeople who are not interested in management and training. The methods here are essential, but foundational. You won't read any advanced closing methods here. If you have a competent sales manager, most of what's in this book should be part of your skill set by the end of your third month with the company.

Also, if you keep jumping from one company to another you'll never gain any momentum in your career. So, if you are with your third sales company this year, chances are, I can't help you.
Most salespeople don't jump from company to company because they were just "too amazing" for the last three companies.

If you are the Sales Manager or CEO

If you have been managing a group of salespeople for more than a day there are several things you already know:

- New people have fears that are unwarranted and will never actually materialize.

- New people have expectations that are unrealistic.

- Without direction, new people will go in a thousand different directions, almost none of them resulting in sales.

New people's fears.
They are afraid of rejection, afraid they won't make money, and afraid of whatever their non-salesperson relatives told them about selling. Sometimes, they are afraid to ask someone to buy. There are ways to kill these fears permanently. We'll be talking about them later.

New people's unrealistic expectations.
We've all seen it. A new person, who has never been in sales before, thinks he will be making a million dollars in the first few months. This person is probably going to be shocked to learn that having no skills doesn't make you rich.

I've had new people tell me the first week,
"You know who would buy a thousand of these? The Army. My brother is in the Army…I'll ask him who we talk to".

"I have an appointment with my Uncle this week. He's rich. He'll buy hundreds of these vacuum cleaners to give as gifts".

"I don't need training, this product should sell itself".

And, while the new person is spending the whole week fantasizing about their, "Billion Dollar Deal", they aren't making money. And who do you think they will blame for that?

Like you, I've hired and trained hundreds of new salespeople over the years. I've seen the training programs of maybe a dozen different companies and participated in creating them. All sizes, different products, different clients. One thing I see in common is that whatever the new salesperson is like after the first couple of weeks, is pretty much what they will be like the rest of their time with your company. Habits are formed, work ethic is established, and the way they view you and the company is pretty well set.

So, if you want to help the rep form good work habits…those habits need to be established from the very beginning. The reps attitude toward the company, how they work with the home office, how they follow procedures, and how they think of their manager, all gets established in the first few weeks.

The purpose if this book is to establish the good work habits that make for a salesperson that will earn a good living, help you lower turnover, and make managing them as painless as possible.

This is a foundational book. This information will set a framework in the new salesperson's mind, that you can then build upon. My goal is to make your job easier, and make the new salesperson's first month far more productive.

May I suggest you get a print copy for all your new sales hires? You'll see why as you read this book. I've priced the book low, for this very purpose. And I kept the book short, to make it more likely to get read.

This book is not meant to replace anything the company is doing. This book is written to take away many of the roadblocks that keep a new rep from being successful, and to make the manager's job easier.

And if you are the new rep reading this part…Congratulations. Your ambition will be rewarded.

Keep reading.

The next part is about *you*.

"People love to buy. And they love to buy from a knowledgeable, friendly salespeople that can answer their questions. Shopping is an American pastime."

– *Claude Whitacre*

New In Sales? Read This

At the beginning of your sales career you may be offered advice by well meaning non-experts, or you may already have beliefs about selling that are simply not true.

There is a learning curve. It took me ten years before I thought of myself as an expert in selling. And, I improved every year. But all the basics, maybe two thirds of everything I knew, I could have learned the first month in selling. I didn't have a great sales manager that provided training tools. I wasn't shown how to close sales. Heck, I didn't even know how to fill out an agreement if someone decided to buy.

So, when I trained new salespeople, I didn't want to repeat the mistakes that were made when I was new in selling.

There are myths you may believe right now about what selling is, and how selling works. Have you watched movies with salespeople in them? 'Glengarry Glen Ross', 'Boiler Room', even the movie about Jordon Belfort titled, 'The Wolf Of Wall Street'….all these movies show salespeople at their worst. The vast majority of successful salespeople don't act like anything you'll see in a movie.

Ask anyone on the street to say what pops in their mind when you say the word "Salesman". You'll hear…con man, high pressure, shifty, liar, pushy…and it goes on from there. But does that really describe salespeople? Only the worst of the bunch. And movies tend to perpetuate that image.

But this image is false. Great salespeople can earn a higher income than anyone else in their company. Their clients and customers trust their recommendations. Selling is helping people decide to do what's in their best long term interest. And if you are working for a great company, many times, what is in the prospect's best interest is allowing you to help them with your product or service. We'll talk more about this a little later.

Why are you in sales?

People decide to go into sales for many reasons. Let's start with things you'll avoid:

Most selling isn't hard physical work. Very few salespeople get injured on the job. Retired salespeople still have all their fingers. You probably won't have to put up with terrible smells, toxic gas, falling from heights, being hit by a piece of construction equipment. You won't have to work outside in sub zero temperatures, or work in attics in the heat of Summer. In short, you'll avoid the bad stuff.

What are some of the benefits of being in sales?

You are always in demand. Salespeople bring business into companies. In every economy more business is needed.

Your skill can grow as you learn more about how to sell. You are studying human nature. And that knowledge will help you in every facet of your life.

Your pay won't be limited to an hourly rate. In almost every case, you will be incentivized to bring in more business. That means you'll get paid what you are worth to the company, not the minimum they think you'll accept. In many companies, the best salesperson earns more money than the CEO. Why? Because he brings in more business than the CEO.

You can be rewarded with vacations, travel, bonuses, and contests. In growing companies…all contests are sales contests. And awards are given to top salespeople. You are acknowledged for your accomplishments.

And, there are other rewards besides money and awards. You are helping people benefit and grow.

When you are talking to a prospect about your offer, you are informing them about options. You are adding a source of supply. If they own a business you are helping that business grow. If you are talking to consumers, you are showing them a better way, and a better experience.

I'll let you in on a secret, people love to buy. And, they love to buy from a knowledgeable, friendly salesperson who can answer their questions. Shopping is an American pastime. Few things in life make a person happier than buying something brand new that they really wanted. You can be there, providing that feeling, every day.

Everyone gets into sales for a different reason, but here is my story…

When I was a teenager, I lived in a very small rural town in Ohio. In that town was a man that wore a nice suit. He was the only person in town that I ever saw wearing a suit and hat, so he stuck out. He was an insurance agent for Mutual Of Omaha. My only experience with insurance was from watching Mutual Of Omaha's Wild Kingdom on TV. It was a nature show.

All I knew was, he wore a suit, drove a nice car, and was friendly. I wanted to be like him.

So, as soon as I turned 21, I was interviewed at the local Mutual Of Omaha office. They rejected me. I went to work for another insurance company, worked hard, and did very well. A few years later, a man showed me a very expensive vacuum cleaner. I bought it, went to work with the company, and did very well….well enough to set sales records, be the Keynote speaker at the annual convention and speak to crowds of salespeople across the country.

Now, about 40 years later, I wish I could go back to see that insurance man, that started it all…and thank him.

It's been a good ride.

"Sales is the only activity in a business that contributes to profit. Everything else contributes to cost."

– Claude Whitacre

Chapter 1

So.....What Is Selling...Really?

I've talked to hundreds of high producing salespeople. You can define "selling" a few different ways. I prefer, "Selling is clear communication, which makes the best decision obvious to the prospect". The fact is, a confused prospect always says, "No". So you have to be clear in your language, and in how you describe your offer. It is your obligation to provide the best information, the information that applies to them, so your prospect can make the most informed decision.

This certainly isn't the only book on selling that you should read. The author of, <u>How To Master The Art Of Selling</u>, Tom Hopkins says selling is "Helping people benefit and grow". I agree.

Sales is the only activity in a business that contributes to profit. Everything else contributes to cost.

The great salesman and sales trainer, Zig Ziglar said, "You get everything you want out of life, if you just help enough other people get what they want". And, *selling*, is giving people what they want.

Tom Hopkins also said, "Selling is the highest paid hard work, and the lowest paid easy work".

I understand why he said it, but I disagree. Imagine a day selling. If it's completely unproductive, if you make no calls, talk to no prospects (or just one), the day drags on forever. It's drudgery. You get drained of energy.

Now, think of a day where you really put forth the effort. You talk to dozens of people, make calls, present your offer, and make a sale or two. How do you feel at the end of that day? Exhilarated! Pumped up! The day just flew by.

I'm going to let you in on a little secret. A productive day builds momentum because the next day you aren't starting from the beginning. You are building on the previous day. Do you know the hardest time to make a call? If you have wasted the day, and it's your first call.

Do you know the easiest time to make a call? Right after you made the first call. You're warmed up, ready, prepared. You are in the Flow.

So, my experience is....once you get in the flow of real effort and real production, it's actually easier to continue than it is to stop and goof off.

"Selling is helping people decide to do what's in their best long term interest."

– *Claude Whitacre*

Chapter 2

What Is A Great Salesperson?

Of the salespeople I know earning a mid-six figure income, they are all trustworthy....meaning that they have earned the customer's trust.

If you are untrustworthy, how many repeat sales do you think you'll make?

That's right, none.

How many referrals will you get if the customer is treated badly?

Again, none.

Great salespeople keep their word. Did you promise delivery on a certain date? Did you say you would call them back in an hour? You'd better do it. Why? If someone promises something, and doesn't deliver...what do you think of them? You know you can't count on them. In some instances, you may even look for a different supplier. Well, your customers think the same way.

The greatest salespeople don't exaggerate claims.

They go for the clearest communication, not the most boastful promises.

Think of the last experience you've had with a great salesperson...one that answered all your questions, made you comfortable with your decision, and acted in a professional way. She wasn't born that way. It took time to develop the habits, the attitude, and the knowledge to make sales as effortless as possible.

Study salespeople you meet. What makes you like them? What turns you off? Use these feelings as a guide to help you know how to approach selling.

Chapter 3

How Your Sales Manager Can Make You Money.

When you start with a company, you are not alone.

Think of your sales manager as "Training wheels" Your sales manager has the experience to save you lots of time in your learning curve. Do what she says until you know more than she does. Her job is to help you make more money. So it's a win-win.

Sales is the only occupation where the manager's goals, the CEO's goals, and your goals…are in alignment.

The company wants the salesperson to make a huge income, so that the company makes a huge profit.

The company may build a product, but salespeople are what build the company.

Chapter 4

Beginner Myths That New Salespeople Believe, And The Reality Behind Them.

Most new salespeople fail in their sales career. It's a fact. Just like 80% of all businesses fail within the first 5 years. But there are reasons for this failure.

After 40 years of personal selling, and 35 years of training salespeople, I have heard just about every idea a new person has, that prevents them from selling.

These are myths. Some of these, you may be thinking yourself. Some may sound silly to you. But, to a new salesperson they sound perfectly valid.

Understanding that these ideas are simply wrong, and why they are wrong, will multiply your chances of a successful sales career. Let's get started;

"I won't be able to sell because I have no experience"

Nobody had experience when they started selling. And new salespeople have a huge advantage. I noticed, when I was brand new, that people wanted to help me. They would be patient if I didn't have a ready answer to their questions. And at least half of the people you talk with, are pulling for you to be successful. They want to help you get started in your career. Don't hide the fact that you are new. It may be the first thing you say…..not as an excuse, but so they are pulling for you to succeed.

"The market is saturated. Nobody will buy"

Is anyone making sales in your industry? If they are then the market isn't saturated. There is a huge advantage to selling a very familiar brand for a familiar company. Much of the selling is already done, before you get there.

If the prospect is familiar with your company, or even your industry, that familiarity adds to their comfort in dealing with you. They feel safer if they know something about what you sell. Even if they heard something bad about your industry, or about your company….that makes you real in their mind.

It gives credibility.
Always use what you have. If you are new, use that. If you are short, use that. If they have never heard of your product, use that.

"Nobody has heard of our product".

For a couple of decades, I sold a product for a company that was not well known. And occasionally, someone would say, "I never heard of your company". And I would say, "That's because they don't advertise. Our business is mostly from referrals and repeat sales to satisfied customers. The company knew that by advertising, it would add substantially to your cost. Aren't you glad they didn't spend that money on advertising so we could pass the savings on to you?"

"I'm not outgoing. I'm introverted. I don't think I can sell"

Being outgoing isn't an asset in selling. This idea comes from the movies. Loud, fast talking salesmen….are products of fiction. Are you shy? Introverted? Listen to this;

When I was in high school, I was so introverted I never went to a sports game, never went to a dance, didn't go to the prom, and I didn't even attend my own graduation.

How did I overcome my shyness? I didn't. I just studied how selling works. Selling is about clear communication. It's about answering questions, and fitting the offer to the prospect. It's more engineering than personality.

You do not have to be outgoing. But you do have to be ambitious.

Ben Feldman was the world's greatest life insurance salesperson. His sales production was mythic. He was so shy, that every year, when he gave a speech to the life insurance convention of million dollar salespeople (MDRT, a group of the greatest producers)…he had to stand behind a screen on stage. He couldn't face the audience. Being shy isn't a problem. Being lazy is.

"I don't think I could ever sell anything"

I don't hear this from salespeople, but from people who are looking for a career. I may ask them if they have ever told their friends about a movie they liked. That's selling. Making recommendations that you know will help someone…is selling. When you bought a new car, didn't you show it off a little? Did you explain all the options you got? That's selling. Giving information in a clear way, is the backbone of selling.

People say they cannot sell when they are doing it every day. It's because they don't want to do...*what they think selling is*. They don't want to pressure people, misrepresent, abuse friendships, sell shoddy products and services. That's what they don't want to do. But selling isn't any of those things.

"But I'm not a born salesman, like you"

When a new salesperson watches an experienced salesperson make a sale, it seems like something they could never do. To many, it seems impossible. A new sales rep once told me, "I could never do as well as you". So I asked him, "Can you drive a car?" Of course he could. "Do you think I can drive a car better than you ever could?". He said, "No. I'm a very good driver".
I said, "Do you remember when you couldn't drive, and it was all a mystery to you? How long did it take for you to learn to drive a car?"

He said, "Just a few weeks". And I said, "It's the same with anything. It looks like magic…until you know how it's done. A few weeks from now, you'll hear a new person say the same thing to you… 'I'm not a born salesperson like you'". It's just a little practice, a little experience, and you are well on your way.

"My product is too….heavy, light, expensive, loud, complex, simple, ugly, whatever"

For years, I sold a vacuum cleaner that weighed 28 pounds. That's darn heavy, for a vacuum cleaner. The first thing I would do, when presenting it, is have the prospect pick it up. "Is that going to be too heavy for you to pick up?"

Almost always they would just pick it up, and say, "No, it's not too heavy to carry". And nobody brought up its weight again.

But I would talk to other reps, and they thought it was a big problem. Why? Because they made it a big problem, when in fact, it wasn't.

"Nobody has any money. Nobody is buying anything"

I actually hear that from salespeople. But I have some evidence to the contrary. What percentage of a person's income, generally gets spent? It hovers right around 100%.

It doesn't matter what they do for a living, or how much they get paid. People tend to spend every cent that comes through their bank account. In fact, our entire population has a name.

We are called "Consumers". Why? Because we spend money. We spend so much money, that many people do it as a hobby. It's popular, and socially required, that we say that we can't buy something, because we don't have the money. But beer sales aren't hurting. The bars are still full on weekends. And, the price of gasoline only slightly effects how people travel.

Of course, the poorest people don't have any disposable income. But they don't, no matter how bad the economy is.

A related myth is; **"Our product is too expensive. Everyone buys based on price"**

Only beginner salespeople believe this, or unsuccessful ones. The truth is, maybe 20% of any market is motivated primarily by the price they pay. The rest are motivated to buy by other factors; the relationship with the salesperson, the quality of what they buy, the company's reputation for service, and other factors.

One way to guarantee that you are only dealing with price shoppers, (The one thing you do not want) is to keep saying that, "We're the cheapest". If your company just advertises that it has the lowest price, you'll only attract the "Lowest price shopper". And they are the least profitable 20% to sell to.

If your company has a higher quality product or service, you are in luck, because these are easier to sell to the widest share of the market.

This next one may seem unbelievable now, but I've seen it too much, not to include it here;

"I'm making too much money. Something has to be wrong with what I'm doing"

If you are used to getting paid hourly, and you suddenly earn a large commission check, it can be daunting.

You may begin to wonder if you really deserve this success. You do. Selling, especially when you are getting paid by commission, is a profession that rewards you in direct proportion to the service you render to customers. The harder you work, the more you learn, the more money you deserve.

In my industry (I sold in prospect's homes), the myth's were;

1) The prospects would buy later, ("I swear on a stack of Bibles that I will buy from you next Tuesday") They are going to buy….. next Tuesday, when their insurance settlement comes in, when they get a raise, when they pay off their truck. You go on Tuesday and they say, "Well, come back at the end of the month". And salespeople would still believe that they had a sure sale…just waiting to buy. But, they never did.

2) You didn't need to see both husband and wife together. Remember, I sold in people's homes. The wife (or husband) would say, "Go ahead, if I like it, I can go ahead and buy it myself. I make the decisions". It actually took me over a year to stop believing it. After analyzing my sales figures, I realized that I had a 2% chance of making a sale if both spouses weren't there to see the presentation. I had a 50% chance of a sale if they were both there. If they were single, they also had a 50% probability of buying.

3) The huge phantom sale in bulk. I called it, 'The Big Deal Time Suck'. A new rep would know someone that works in an industry, or for the government, or had a franchise…and the fantasy was, "If I can just sell 10,000 of these to the owner of Disney World, I can retire". But we sold at retail, not wholesale. And our product was used in homes, not industry. But it didn't matter. If the new rep got this idea stuck in their head, they would waste weeks planning for the big sale, ignoring all the sales that they could make right now, to pay their bills.

Maybe your company sells to industry, or businesses. Maybe your 'Big Deal Time Suck' looks like this; "I have a friend, who knows a guy, that used to live next door to Donald Trump. If I can get in with Trump, I'll make a fortune. " Maybe….but not your first week.

I couldn't break new people of these beliefs. I just had to let them find out for themselves. The "We'll absolutely, definitely, buy later…and we'll pay in cash" dead ends would take the longest to learn. Sometimes reps would still be chasing these phantom sales months after they started.

By the way, some sales do take more than one visit. Your manager will be able to tell you if that's the norm. Just don't delude yourself into thinking "pretending to sell" is actually selling.

Chapter 5

Essential Methods To Build A Foundation In Your Sales Career

Buy what you sell.
Do you sell a product or service that is used by most people? Then you need to buy what you sell. Very soon after you start selling you'll be asked by prospects what you use.

You'll be asked if you own what you sell. In every instance, your answer will either help or hurt your chance at a sale. And don't lie. There are a thousand unconscious signals you give off when you lie. And most are visible on your face and in your body language.

If you're lucky, buying what you sell may even count in generating sales commissions and count for contests. If not, your brother needs one. Buy it for him and borrow it forever.

If you sell to businesses, does your business use what you are selling?

When you are talking to customers, there are several questions running through their minds. Here is one of the most important;

"Who else bought this and is using this?"

If you have a list of customers (or your company's list) Great! But you need to believe in what you sell. And the best and quickest way to establish that belief is by buying what you sell.

I know life insurance salespeople who own no life insurance. Really? How can they justify someone buying something that they wouldn't buy themselves?

The truth is, they don't really believe in what they sell. And their incomes show it.

Does your company have stock options? Buy stock in your company.

There is more to "Buying what you sell" than just owning the product you sell. Invest in getting to know the people who support your sales efforts. Learn the history of your company, your industry, your product or service. You'll be amazed how often this information will help answer a customer's question.

Help build your company's Brand. Sure, you are helping your company, but you are helping yourself even more. A Brand gives a sense of permanence to your offer…a sense of security, reliability…it shows the customer that they have someone to turn to, if you quit.

I always told the customer that the company treats me well. What are they thinking when you say your company treats you well? They are thinking, "Good. If they treat him well, they'll treat me well too".

I was going to buy a new car from a salesman on a car lot. I asked, "How does the dealership treat you here?"

I swear this is true. He said "My manager is a drunk, the company keeps cheating me out of commissions, I hate working here". Now, what do you think that made me think? It made me think, "I don't want to buy from this guy, because he's a whiner. And I certainly don't want to buy from this dealership. If they treat their salespeople badly, how will they treat me?"

If you have a concern with your company, always bring it up, in private, to your manager. Never talk about it to the customer. It kills your sales.

I own a few businesses. A retail store, a speaking business, and I sell local online marketing services to brick and mortar business owners. When I'm presenting my service to a business owner, they ask, "Do you use this service yourself?" Of course, I do. In fact, it's the main way I promote my store, and the main way I get leads for my local online marketing services. I practice what I preach. Do you practice what you preach? That's what prospects want to know.

And if you use what you sell, you can give a review on review websites. You can tell how you use it. You can describe the benefits from first-hand experience.

In my retail store, we sell vacuum cleaners. If a customer says, "What do you use at home?" I can show them. I can explain why we decided on it. To the customer you aren't selling as much as giving your opinion.

If at all possible, buy what you sell.

Know your competition.
High earning salespeople know their competition.. I hear from salespeople, "We have no competition, we're the best". Maybe that's true. But until the customer knows that, you have lots of competition in their mind. And you just saying, "We're better than them", isn't going to be enough. A thorough read through of their company brochure, should tell you enough. Or a side by side comparison of your offers would be enough. But, when someone asks you how you compare to a competitor the statement, "I don't know", will not help you make that sale.

In fact, if the prospect asks you a question, that you don't know the answer to, it kills the momentum of that sale. Why? Because no matter what you say after that, the person is still thinking about that question they asked, that you couldn't answer.
So, know who else sells what you sell. Know their strong and weak points.

And if they ask about your competition, <u>this is vital</u>…don't just slam your competitor. It always sounds untrue to the prospect. I always say a few nice things about my competition, and then show the advantages of what I have. And never lie about a competitor. If for no other reason than…you have no idea what the person you are talking to already knows.

This is all especially important if your prospect already owns a competitive product. Never say anything bad about what the person has bought in the past. This is a sure sales killer. Never criticize a past buying decision. Compliment their past buying decisions. Why? Because that's what you're going to ask them to do again….with you.

Chapter 6

The Fastest Way To See Sales Made.

Ask to ride with an experienced rep. Make sure this person is the most successful person in the office. A week should do it. Continue training in the office. Read your sales manual, company brochures, and study your presentation, if you have one. But you will benefit greatly, by tagging along on sales calls with an experienced successful rep. Your manager may fill this position.

But remember, you are going with them to watch them sell. They aren't going with you, to watch you sell. That comes later.

Do NOT make calls with a rep just because you like them. You don't need a buddy. You need a teacher. And that teacher can only teach you what they know.

If you tag along with a rep that sells in low volume, all he can teach you is to sell in low volume.

The rules when tagging along;

You have to make it worth the rep's time. She's doing you a favor. You are not helping her sell. She is helping you learn. Offer to carry things, and buy the coffee. If she is making prospecting calls on the phone, ask if you can record a few calls.

Do not ask for part of her commission. She is doing you a favor.

Use the restroom before you go on a call. Asking to excuse yourself in the middle of a presentation destroys the momentum of the sales process. And now, the prospect is wondering where you are and what you are doing. Trust me. Use the restroom before you go on an appointment.

Promise to keep quiet while she is selling. Nothing you can add will help them in a sales presentation. I've seen sales destroyed because the new guy said the wrong thing. I've seen new guys argue with the experienced rep, in front of the buyer. Never do that. It will kill the sale.

The benefit you get is that you'll see that selling isn't unpleasant. Nobody really yells at you or is mean to you. Selling is a completely natural act. You need to see how it's done, and how easy it can be. When you are brand new to sales, nearly everything you think you know about selling is wrong. Much of high level selling is counter-intuitive. Ask questions after you leave the sales call. But never ask the rep questions while in front of the customer. It side tracks the entire sales effort.

When I give speeches to sales groups, I get this question, "What's the most important thing to consider when training new people?". My answer is, "They need to see sales actually being made."

New salespeople may not even believe that people buy, what they are selling. They need to know, in their very core, that it's normal for prospects to buy from them…that sales are the expected result of sales calls. They can only get that certainty by seeing real sales being made in front of them. They need to see the flow of business, how it works, what to expect.

Riding with an experienced rep, seeing sales being made, will smooth out the rough edges of the new person's fears. And they will become a salesperson who expects sales. And, as a business owner that had salespeople working for him, I can promise you, the new people that expect to sell, are going to make more sales.

Chapter 7

How To Overcome Your Fear Of Rejection.

New people have fears that experienced salespeople do not.

I've had new salespeople think that prospects were going to yell at them, be aggressive, maybe even threaten them. Why? Because of the way salespeople are portrayed in movies. But the truth is, nearly everyone is polite, and respectful. At least they are civil. In my experience of giving over 12,000 sales presentations in people's homes…I've been asked to leave twice. Both times, my fault.

New people have an exaggerated fear of rejection.

Non-salespeople think of rejection as personal. So, a new salesperson will see rejection as personal. But in business, it isn't personal at all. Think of your own experience. You ask someone out on a date, they make up an excuse, and you feel bad. Why? Because they are judging you as a person. It is you that is being rejected.

But in business, and in sales, rejection isn't personal. They are saying "No" to your idea, your product, your service…but it has nothing to do with you personally.

In my seminars, I may have someone come to the front of the room, and ask everyone in the front row…one at a time…if they like butterscotch. Some say yes, some say no.

When we have seen this done with maybe 10 people in the front row, I'll ask the participant, "Five people said they liked butterscotch, but 5 people said they didn't. How do you feel about the people who liked butterscotch? How about the people who don't like it?". Invariably, they don't feel any different about the two groups. Why? Because it isn't personal. Even *liking* butterscotch isn't personal.

Now, imagine you sell butterscotch. Now, does it bother you? Probably not. Why? Because the people that don't buy your butterscotch, just don't like butterscotch. It has nothing to do with you as a person.

The other extreme, naïve expectations.

New people can also get so excited about their new position, their new offer, that they have expectations that are sure to be dashed. For example, I've seen new people make a few sales, and then they run into a few non-buyers, and it ruins them. They believed that their offer was so amazing that everyone would buy. But, everyone doesn't buy. And seeing how an experienced rep handles that situation, will go far, to help the new rep see how selling really works, and how people really react to the sales presentations.

Finding out that there is a competitor with a lower price, faster delivery, different position in the market…can also take a new person by surprise.

"In your town, this very moment, there are between ten and a hundred people that are looking to buy exactly what you sell. And they will say "Yes" to your offer without much effort at all. You just need to find them."

– Claude Whitacre

Chapter 8

The Single Biggest Theat To Your Success, And How To Avoid It.

Don't Hang Out With The Losers

In every company there are some really active, productive, working salespeople...that are making real money. And there are many more, that are barely getting by.

You'll be able to spot them right away. They don't work hard, and they always blame someone else for their failure, usually the company. They hang out together, and will do activities all day that have nothing to do with selling. The unpopular guy, the one that's always out selling and breaking company records...that's who you talk to.

If a guy walks up to you on your first day, and says, "New guy, let me tell you how it works around here"....chances are, he's not the top rep.

In the mid-1970s, a group of us local insurance salesman would meet at the Perkin's Pancake House in the morning for coffee. There were maybe 10 of us. We met at 9AM. By 9:30, I would be leaving for my first appointment. There was one other guy who would also leave to work. We would go on separate appointments. During the day, between appointments, we would stop back at the Perkin's. Yup....All 8 of the other guys would still be there, drinking coffee. I'm sure they told their wives that they were working.

My friend and I would describe the sales we just made, and how many referrals we got. After a short break, off we would go again, on another appointment.

These men would talk about the weather, politics, which company was better, the economy, and they talked about problems they had at home. But never about the sale they just made, or the appointment they were going on. To a brand new salesperson, they would be indistinguishable from productive salespeople. A new person could talk to them about selling for hours, and think they were talking to a great salesperson. But eventually, they would notice that the agent never actually went on an appointment…never actually made an effort. And the new guy would be ruined.

But they actually will teach you something…..

They will teach you why "not selling" is OK, and why it isn't your fault you aren't selling. They would teach you how to waste an entire day, while pretending that you are working. They would teach you who to blame, for your lack of sales.

They may even teach you how to pad your expense account, to raise some easy cash. Or how to fake sales records so it looks like you're working, when you aren't.

Don't blame them. Everyone in the huddle has been lied to by the untrained salespeople in the huddle before them. They are just passing down this useless information to the next generation.

When you meet an experienced salesperson, ask a few questions. Pay attention to their answers. What sales results are they getting? Are they getting the results you want to get? If not, then why in the world are you listening to them?

The mating cries of the loser salesperson……

"Our prospects only care about price"

"Our competitor sells exactly what we do, for less"

"Our competition is better known than we are"

"People want what we don't have in stock (or services we don't offer)"

"The market is down right now. Nobody is buying"

"We are in a small town, and don't have a big market"

"We are in a big city, and we have too much competition"

"Our local economy is bad"

"People just don't know our brand. We need more advertising"

If you hear this from a group of salespeople, you are sitting at the wrong table.

When I was 22 years old, I started selling life insurance for an old, respected company. The office I worked out of was one of the lowest producing offices in the country. But I was new, young, eager to succeed, and didn't know any better…so I worked my tail off.

In my first full calendar year, I was the third top salesperson with the company of 2,200 agents.. I knew very little. I simply worked hard. If I remember correctly, there were 14 or 15 agents in that office, and a few sales managers. There were months, where my production was more than the rest of the office combined. Am I telling you this to brag? Maybe a little. But here is what you need to know about it.

They hated me. The other agents would hide my car, hide my check, wouldn't let me go to lunch with them. One other agent there, the most productive one, explained it to me. He said, "Claude, the reason they hate you is because, at every weekly sales meeting, when we all give our results for the week, it is clear that you and I are the only ones really working. And you're setting sales records that rub that fact in their faces. They don't want to be reminded that people buy insurance, sales are possible, and it just takes a little work. You are the evidence of their sloth. So, they hate you. Don't worry. They hate me too".

Frankly, it didn't help that I was young and aggressive. I wasn't subtle about how much money I made, or how much I sold. I acted like a jerk, and paid the price. I remember one week, I bought a new briefcase, and stuffed it with all the policies I had to deliver that week. It was full. At the sales meeting, I dumped it all over the table at the front of the room….just to make a point.

Truly, I thought I was motivating them. I wanted them to make money too. I was too young to know that they didn't want to be motivated. They wanted to be insulated away from sales, in the comfort of their inactivity. They weren't bad people, just not ambitious people.

The next week, one of the agents, a lovely older lady, handed me a copy of **How To Win Friends And Influence People**. She was gracious about it, but I got the message.

Sell a ton, but you don't have to be a jerk about it.

Post Script; I didn't know where to put this, so I put it here. If you are talking to a salesperson, and you ask them how they are doing, they tend to complain, "I'm doing as well as anyone in this bad economy". And if you go on an appointment with one of them, listen to how they talk afterwards. It doesn't matter whether they sell or not, it's how they react to it. Did they blame the prospect? "That guy was too stupid to buy". Or, did they blame the company? "Another sale went to XYZ company. How does our company expect us to sell with this competition?". In other words, they blame something other than themselves. They aren't learning from the missed sale. Now, if they say, "Did you see where I missed the sale?" or "What can we learn from that?" you may have a winner. Every missed sale is a teaching moment. Value what you can learn.

And if they make a sale, how do they react? Do they act like it's a rare event to be celebrated? I was in a car with a salesman who had just made a sale. He cranked up the music, and started singing loudly. He wanted to go out and celebrate. My first thought was, "He must not make sales very often". If I took a new person with me, and I made a sale, I would ask things like, "Why do you think they bought? What need did our product fill? I almost lost the sale. Do you know when that was?". I want the sale to be a teaching moment.

"People say they cannot sell, when they are doing it every day. It's because they don't want to do...*what they think selling is.*"

– Claude Whitacre

Chapter 9

The Best Way To Build A Sales Career.

Stay With The Company You Are With

The grass is always greener on the other side of the fence. Why? Because you aren't looking closely. As long as your company keeps its promises to you, and provides a great product or service, you will always be better off staying with that company.

Sales Legends aren't born by moving from company to company. If you want to be at the top, it takes sustained effort. And changing companies, even in the same industry, breaks that chain of effort.

And, truth be told, some people buy from you …because of the company you represent. If my life insurance guy changes companies, he loses me as a client… because I won't change companies.

Reputations are killed by moving around. The longer you stick with a company that keeps its word, the more momentum you build with your customers. Longevity with a company builds trust in the mind of customers. Every time you tell a customer that you changed companies, you have to explain why. And every reason to change companies sounds bad to the buyer. It either makes you look bad, or makes the company look bad. Neither one helps your cause. And every time you change companies…you have to resell the idea of buying from you, and you have to sell the new company brand. All that trust and reliability they had with the last company? That's gone, if the customer leaves with you.

And to the buyer, if you leave one company, it's possible that it's the company's fault. If you move twice, it's because of you. You're the problem. That's what they will think. You don't want that reputation.

If you stay with the same company your chances of getting referrals and repeat buyers are increased. These relationships you develop make selling far easier and far more fun. When you leave, all of this momentum is gone. Everything you built with the company? Gone.

The benefits of staying with one company for the long haul;

Chances for advancement in the company increase over time. The president of your company has probably been there for decades. She probably wasn't hired as the "new guy" and just made president. Most managers and trainers are promoted from within. "Loyalty to the company" is considered when promotions are given.

Your reputation with customers is enhanced. When you are with a company for a long time, the customers tend to think two things; The company is keeping you, because you're a good guy…and you are staying with the company because it's a good company. You may even want to remember to say that sometime. The words "Steady" and "Trustworthy" come to mind, when discussing a salesperson that has stayed with their company for the long haul.

Sales get easier with referrals and repeat sales. And repeat sales and referrals dry up, if you change companies. Why do customers refer others to do business with you? They refer others when you treat them really well, deliver on your promises, prove yourself to be reliable, and are proven to be trustworthy. These attributes take time to establish. They form your reputation.

Your knowledge of how your company works, makes selling easier. Every time you change companies, there is a learning curve. And every time you change companies, that learning curve starts all over again.

By staying with the same company, relationships are formed in the company that will help you sell, and aid in job promotions.

Job security increases over time. If changes in staff are inevitable, the newer people tend to be let go or transferred first. If your company offers benefits like hospitalization and retirement benefits, that may go away if you leave.

Starting over, always starts with Zero. Bloom where you are planted.

I know it sounds like I'm repeating myself here. I wanted to hit this idea from every angle…to really drill the idea home. It's that important.

Chapter 10

The Best Tool A Company Can Give You To Guarantee Your Sales

Practice your prepared presentation.

Some companies have a prepared presentation that you need to study. And some companies sell products and services that do not lend themselves to an organized presentation. For example, a wholesaler selling hundreds of different products.

But if you sell a product or service that is sold with a standardized presentation you are doing yourself a great service if you learn it thoroughly.

When I was training salespeople, I would pass out the presentation for them to learn. Invariably, someone would say, "I sell better without a prepared script". Sometimes they were one of the brighter people there. And, because I am primarily a salesman myself….I understood why they were saying that. But it's a flawed idea that "winging it" works better.

Most prepared sales presentations didn't just get written on a whim. Usually, a lot of thought and testing went into it. Even the words were tested to see which were more effective.

The presentation I used was tested over years of trial and error. I kept what worked, and threw out what didn't. I learned the best sequence with which to show our product, the best questions to ask, and the how to save time by answering common questions in the presentation.

So, I would explain to "Mister wing it", "Have you ever seen a movie scene that made you cry? Do you think the actors were winging it? Have you ever watched a stand-up comedian perform, and get a standing ovation? Do you think he just started winging it, as he got on stage? No. These people were prepared. They knew what they needed to say, the best order to say it in to get the reaction they wanted."

I have also told new people that they were welcome to change anything in the presentation they wanted, as long as they tried my presentation first. If they wanted to change something, just run it by me. Why? because the customer needs a clear picture of what we offer. I need to know that the rep is telling them everything they need to know. Winging it created gaps in understanding. I would tell the reps, "If you follow the standardized presentation, I'll know what you told the customer if they call". Service problems and misunderstandings are kept to a minimum.

If the company has a planned presentation, use it. You'll soon begin to see how every part of the presentation works to build the sale and speed up the selling process. Eventually, you may not use the company presentation. But to discard it because, "It's just not me", is like an actor saying "Shakespeare? I'll wing it".

By the way, even if you do not have a prepared presentation to learn, you may still have a short sequence of facts that are more effective if said in a certain way. For example, the way you explain warranties, service, training, shipping, ordering procedures, explaining contracts. Clarity of communication is what you are looking for. Much of this can be found in your company brochures.

Use company visual aids. Company visual aids, if provided, establish credibility in the mind of the consumer. You look more solid if you have company visual aids. A presentation with visuals will keep you and the prospect on track toward the sale. It will make sure most of the prospect's questions are answered before they become objections. A company prepared presentation adds credibility to your company and in you. Sharp looking visual aids create a sense of "Permanence" in your customer's vision of your company. They look more "Official" than a presentation without visual aids. Not using your visual aids is like having a hammer and saying " I can put that nail in better myself" and just throwing the hammer away. Your visual aids are tools. They make your job easier.

And keep your materials crisp and clean. Everything you do, in front of a prospect, everything they see…effects how they see you. Crumpled applications, old spec sheets, messy briefcase…all shows the prospect that you are not expecting them to buy. Be prepared, because someone is going to buy from you.

If the company has demonstration aids, use them.

A friend of mine owned a mattress store. He would explain to customers how the mattresses were made. One day I asked if the company had ever thought of creating a cross section of a high end mattress, to show the quality. He said, "Sure, it's in the back room. I never use it".

Demonstration tools are your best tools.

A demonstration destroys buying objections. It clarifies the thinking of the prospect. It offers them proof that what you are saying is true. "Seeing is believing" is really true. Have you ever watched an infomercial? The entire show is a demonstration. The product is used in front of the camera, features are shown, uses are demonstrated. Why? Because it works. You've heard, "A picture is worth a thousand words"? Well, a good demonstration is worth a thousand pictures.

A good demonstration aid can do much of the work of explaining your offer. It can do much of the heavy lifting.

I own a retail store (at the time of this writing). Some of my products can do amazing things. Demonstrations make the unbelievable…believable. Demonstration materials prove what you are saying. The customer can see, hear, and touch what you are talking about…if you use your demonstration aids. You may think you are saving time by not using what the company provides, but that's a mistake…. A beginner mistake. Use everything you have. You never know what that one thing will be, that gets the sale.

Literally, every day, I get people buying from me, when they already saw the same thing for less in another city. Why? Because the other guys didn't demonstrate the product. And, demonstrations create a desire to buy that a description simply cannot. What if you sell a service that cannot be demonstrated? You show the results. You show testimonials from satisfied clients. You offer past examples of how your service paid off. You offer proof that what you say…is true. Charts, graphs, comparison sheets, and product/service brochures will help you here.

Chapter 11

The Surest Way To Guarantee Steady Increases In Sales.

Track your sales and sales activities.

Your company may require that you keep certain performance records. This is so they can see where you can use improvement. It's for your benefit as well as theirs.

Whether my company required I keep records or not, I always kept my own records of how I was selling. Records show you where you are and whether you are improving or not.

Keep records of what matters to you. I used to keep records of my sales commissions. I knew where I was by the day, week, and month. I knew if I needed to work harder, or if I could take a day off. This income schedule included the sales calls and presentations. Wouldn't you like to know how much money you earn for every sales call you make, whether they buy or not? How much you earn for every hour of sales activity? Just never lie to yourself. These records are far more powerful as sales motivation than any motivational sales meeting.

For example, when I was selling in people's homes, I kept records on my own sales results, and daily logs of when I worked, and how much I earned on each sale I made.

As a side note, I found that over a three year period, I never went more than eight hours of work, between sales. In other words, every eight hours of actual prospecting and selling, generated at least one sale. Wouldn't you like to know that kind of information? You can get it by keeping accurate records of your sales efforts.

What you measure, you can improve.

Here is why keeping accurate records of your sales activity is so important….

It alerts you when you need improvement. It tells you when something is wrong. It tells you when you are improving. It tells you, if you try a new idea…if this new idea is helping you…or hurting you.

For example, I kept records of where the sale came from. Was it a cold call? Was it a customer referral? Was it a lead the company gave me? After several months of keeping these records, I knew how much a referral was worth, how much a single cold call was worth…and I learned the most profitable ways to prospect. Had I not kept these records, I would really have no idea how to get better results.

Since I was on commission, I also had income goals. Actually "goals" is the wrong word. It was just a schedule that I worked….because I knew how much money I wanted to earn every week.

And if I wanted to raise my income by say $500 that week, I knew exactly what I had to do, in prospecting activity, to guarantee that I made the money. Keeping these detailed records let me know what I had to do!

"I hear from salespeople 'We have no competition, we're the best'. Maybe that's true. But until the customer knows that, you have lots of competition in their mind. And you just saying, 'We're better than them', isn't going to be enough."

– Claude Whitacre

Chapter 12

The Single Best People To Sell To, When You Are Starting Out.

Sell to your warm market.

For every new salesperson, the question comes up… "Should I try to sell to my friends and relatives?"

Of course, if you sell heavy construction equipment, and none of your friends and relatives are in construction…it's easy. No, you don't try to sell them anything.

But, what if you sell something that they might need? Insurance? Real estate? Investments, Appliances? Furniture? Tax services?

Now, what do you do?

When I was selling vacuum cleaners, I didn't bring it up for years. To me, that would be "taking advantage" of our relationship.

One day, my Mother-In-Law called me and asked if I could fix her vacuum cleaner. I drove to her home, and looked at a brand new vacuum cleaner...the same brand I sold. I asked where she got it. She said, "A nice young man showed it to me, and gave me a good deal".
She actually paid more than I charged, but on with the story….
I asked, "Didn't you know that I sold the same brand of vacuum cleaner?" She said, "Sure".
And then I asked, "Why did you buy it from this other guy?"

And she said, "You…never…asked".

I don't know if she was trying to teach me something or not. But I got the lesson. If you sell something that most people will eventually buy….why shouldn't they buy from you?

Who else would you trust to take care of your friends and relative's needs? People want to deal with people they know and trust. Wouldn't you want to buy from someone you know?

If they ever have a problem with the company, who is guaranteed to take their side? Who is guaranteed to look out for your friend's best interests? You.

Some new sales positions ask that you get the names of everyone you know, to start the ball rolling getting leads, sales, and referrals.

My suggestion is to bring it up, but make it super easy to say, "No thanks".

I train new salespeople, and here is what I tell them to do…

Here is an example, "John. I sell life insurance now. I've been reluctant to bring this up, because we are friends. But I've been giving it some thought, and think you may benefit from what I offer. Would you be open to an appointment to talk about it further? If, for any reason, you don't want to…just tell me now, so I can stop thinking about it."

There is no hesitation between the words "further" and "If". It's one run on sentence.

If they are a close friend and know what I do, I'll shorten it to; "Bob, I've been avoiding this for awhile, but it's glaringly obvious that you would benefit from my service. Now, we're friends. If you want to discuss it further, let me know now. If you don't, let me know now. In any event, I can stop stewing over this".

And you know what happens? They usually laugh a little, and say something like, "I was wondering when you'd get around to it. Sure, come on over"

If they really aren't interested, they will say something like, "Well, thank you very much for thinking about me. Now, please pass me the remote". And you don't ask them again.

See? Nobody got mad. Nobody was nervous. Nobody got offended. They just let you know, very nicely, that they were not a good prospect for your offer. And for them, that's the last time I bring it up.

About 20 years after I started selling vacuum cleaners in people's homes….finally…I asked a relative. I asked my Mom for the phone numbers of all my aunts, uncles, cousins, nieces and nephews. It may have been 40 names and phone numbers (the ones that were adults, and local enough to drive to) . I used almost word for word, the second approach I gave you a minute ago, and all but one asked me to stop over. Of course, I gave them all a healthy discount (with some offers, like insurance, you can't). All but one relative bought. I didn't ask for referrals from these guys, because I really gave them a discount that I didn't want to give anyone outside the family.

But it was an incredible month or so.

Personally, I don't get referrals from people who don't buy. But when I started out, I did, and some of them bought. And I never get referrals from someone I gave a deep discount, that I don't want to repeat.

But if you start off by selling to friends and relatives, you very quickly will be selling out of your "Friends and Family" circle. If you get referrals from relatives, even close ones, you'll very quickly be talking to people you never met.

I know reps that have never had to talk to a single stranger, because they talked to people they knew, and got referrals from the ones that bought from them. What a way to live.

Chapter 13

What All Successful Salespeople Have In Common.

Be a selling student. I've been asked about my education. I finished high school. That's it. But my education never stopped.

Here is a reality that I like to point out. When most people graduate from high school, that means they stopped reading and studying when they were 18 years old. A college education usually means they stopped reading and studying when they were 22 or 24 years old. That's the main difference.

And that's a mistake. Anyone who achieved something great, studied, trained, improved over the years. When I talk to salespeople, sometimes they tell me, "I've been selling for 20 years!". But after talking to them, I can see that they have really been doing the same thing for 20 years, without improvement.

When you go to company meetings, talk to the top salespeople. Ask how they prospect. Ask what books they read.

Study books about selling from people who made their fortunes selling, not books by people who think they know what selling should be like. A hundred dollars invested at *Amazon.com* can build you a great sales library. After a year of studying your sales craft, and applying what you learn, you'll be ahead of the rest of the pack, I promise.

Read books about your industry. Read about its history, improvements made, discoveries made. Perhaps much of this is available on your company website or brochures. Study the websites of other suppliers in your industry. There is always something to be learned by this research.

Watch YouTube videos on competing products, sales techniques in your industry, and how your product works. You'll pick up new ideas on presenting your offer.

"Never say anything bad about what the person has bought in the past. This is a sure sales killer. Never criticize a past buying decision. Compliment their past buying decisions. Why? Because that's what you're going to ask them to do again….with you."

– Claude Whitacre

Chapter 14

The First Skill To Learn To Fill Your Pipeline With Buyers.

Get great at prospecting first. When I was hiring and training salespeople, I taught them how to prospect, before how to present the product, or close the sale. Why? Because prospecting is the easiest part of selling, and the least fun. So I would find out very quickly, if prospecting was going to be to irritating to the salesperson. There was no reason to train someone in presentation skills, and closing skills…if prospecting was going to be too stressful for them.

Likely, in the beginning, you'll be doing cold calling, either by phone or in person. Use your company script, if one is available. My book Sales Prospecting, covers the subject in complete detail. But always use your company materials first, before you try to reinvent the wheel.

I always suggest learning how to prospect from the most successful salesperson in your company, or office. Offer to help them for a week or so. Carry their equipment, help them prospect for new business. Don't just ask for a favor, offer to help them. Actually seeing a successful salesperson get results from their prospecting efforts will solidify your confidence that you can do it too.

Do you think I started out working with the top salesperson, learning the fast way, how to sell?

No. Here's what I did, and here's what I learned from that.

At 21, I started selling life insurance. I was licensed…which meant I knew basically how insurance worked…but I knew nothing about selling.

The office had some basic sales aids. A few scripts for cold calling, a basic illustrated sales presentation (completely generic)…and that was it.

I came from a blue collar family. Work was eight hours, two ten minute breaks and a lunch.
I didn't know any better, so I just assumed that's how much you worked. I didn't know about how to waste time, take three hour lunches, and pretend you were working. I just knew how to put in an eight hour day. So, that's what I did.

I knocked on stranger's doors, talking about life insurance. I called strangers out of the phone book. I asked for referrals in such a way to virtually guarantee not to get any. I was really terrible at selling.

All I had on my side was endurance, and eight hours a day. I was incredibly lucky that I found a couple of books written by legendary life insurance salespeople. Ben Feldman…Joe Gandolfo.

Within two months, I was the top salesperson in the office. My first full calendar year, I was the third top guy in the country. (for that company, out of 2,200 agents)

I had no mentor telling me how to sell. I didn't go to training seminars. I got to be the third top salesperson for my company on desire and ambition alone. Why am I telling you this? Because if you have the desire to succeed in sales, that can carry you much of the way.

The information you are holding in your hand this moment? I knew none of this. But there was a secret that I didn't know then, that helped me. I'm going to give it to you right now;

In your town, this very moment, there are between ten and a hundred people that are looking to buy exactly what you sell. And they will say "Yes" to your offer without much effort at all. You just need to find them.

And I just started to learn this lesson, when I was about 23 or 24 years old….. Back in the late 1970's.

Chapter 15

A Guaranteed Way To Get A Sale Right Now, And Win That Contest.

It was a dark and stormy night....

This story is true.

I had just quit selling life insurance a few month before, and switched to selling high end vacuum cleaners. Let's just say I was attracted to shiny objects.

Anyway, I worked for a very well known company. I was in a sales contest, and it was the last day of the month. I had 15 sales that month, and would get a huge bonus (more than the retail price of the vacuum cleaner) if I sold my 16th vacuum that month.

It got to be about 6PM..and the wind started blowing pretty hard. A huge storm was blowing into town, and I needed a sale.

I had no appointments that evening. So, because I just didn't know any better…I started running from house to house. My prepared greeting went out the window. I just blurted out, "Hi, I'm Claude. I sell great vacuum cleaners, and I need a sale tonight. I'll show it to you if you give me your word, if you like what you see, that you will buy from me tonight. I really need a sale"

Honest, that's what I said. This is so long ago, I can't really remember how many doors I knocked on. It seems like it could have been 30 or 35. But one nice guy, said these magic words, "Sure. We've been needing a good vacuum cleaner. If we like what you have, we'll buy it from you"

The storm arrived. At times, I had to yell, because the thunder was so loud.

Yes, they bought.

Thank you, Mister, wherever you are.

Of course, my approach was terrible. But what was worth more to me than that sale…and the bonus…was what I had learned. If you prospect quickly, you'll eventually find a great prospect that will most likely buy from you.

Which brings me to one of your most important lessons in selling;

When you prospect, do it quickly. If you are on the phone, stay on the phone, while dialing the next number. Call as many prospects as you can in the time devoted to prospecting.

Now, why is this important? Momentum. If you delay calling, keep procrastinating, you may dial three numbers in two hours. I've watched it happen. You make no appointments, and declare, "What a waste of time. Nobody is buying".

But, if you give it a solid two hours. Calling maybe 75 prospects in that time. You'll almost certainly have two or three solid appointments. Maybe more. And time will fly, because you are busy. When prospecting, and in selling, speed matters.

If your company offers you a script, use it. If they don't, read the book Sales Prospecting.

Yes, I wrote it.

Which brings us to a principle that I use, that will dramatically improve your chances at being the top rep in your company.

Chapter 16

The Key To Scheduling That Maximizes Sales.

Blocking Time.

Here is a short exercise for you. Do it when you are not supposed to be working. In the evening is great. Figure out the best times to prospect for new business. Decide when you are going to do each activity. Create a schedule, and stick to it.

For example, for years, when I primarily cold called residents at their homes, I discovered times when most people were home. Most were home after 5:30 in the afternoon. So, my prospecting day started then.

During the day, I would train other salespeople, take care of paperwork, do my service calls, read, spend time with my family, and do everything else. But starting at 5:30 precisely, I was either making my first phone call, or knocking on my first door. I worked until 9PM. On Saturday, I started at 11AM, and worked until 4 or 5PM. That's when I stopped prospecting. If I was on a sales call, of course, I finished it.

Selling marketing programs to business owners, I would start calling at 9AM, and would stop at 11AM. But at 9AM, I was dialing out. I wasn't getting my papers ready, fixing a cup of coffee, listening to the news….To me, it was a job. I started working at 9AM. I prospected four days a week, because sometimes I had morning appointments. So I set aside a day for that.

In your industry, do prospects get to work at 7AM? Do you call them at work? Start calling at 7AM. Call fast. Get it done.

What are the most important parts of blocking out your day?
1) Once you set a time, work as though it's a job. Just start.
2) Do the non-selling part of your day, when prospects can't see you. In other words, in non-selling time.

So, how much time a day do you prospect? Enough to keep you busy.

When you are brand new, you have no appointments, no presentations, and no service work, because you have no customers. So, when I started out, all I did was prospect. The whole day.

And even though I had no idea what I was doing, I was so busy that sales just fell into my lap.

As you progress in your sales career, you'll see how much you need to prospect, and the best ways to prospect, to keep your appointment calendar full.

"New salespeople may not even believe that people buy what they are selling. They need to know, in their very core, that it's normal for prospects to buy from them."

– Claude Whitacre

Chapter 17

Fast Start Methods That Will Jump Start Your Career.

Call reluctance...one pushup theory

No matter how exciting your sales career is at this moment, there will be days that you will have trouble picking up the phone, making calls. There will be times when you are just not excited about selling that day. If you have a few of these days in a row, eventually, you'll have a sales slump.

And, in my experience... long term sales slumps are the result of not working.

It's as simple as that.

Every sales person can have a day where they make no sales. Every few years, I'll experience an entire week, where no new sales are made. But more than a week? In my case, that always meant I wasn't working. And in every case, when a rep that worked for me wasn't making sales…it came back to simply not making sales calls and going on appointments.

For a three month period, as an experiment, I had all the reps in my office keep real records of how they spent their day. I didn't care about non-work activity. I wanted to know how many calls they made, how many contacts, how many presentations. And the time spent in each activity.

We quickly found out that each rep had a different income, per hour in front of prospects. But that rep consistently earned the same amount every week…per hour of actual sales effort.

If their income went down for two weeks in a row? We knew that it was because they were working less. Sure, they were arranging their desk, in meetings, talking about the economy, watching training DVDs…but I didn't count any of that. We only counted the actual time spent talking to prospects, or customers. Anyone can have an off day. But if it's an off two weeks? You're creating it.

Now, the questions should be "How do we get motivated to work every day, consistently? How do we make calls when we don't feel like it?"

Me? My best motivation was always a weekly income goal I had. For years, it was $1,000 a week in net income (this was in the 1980's. Now it's much more). I would start on Saturday. Sometimes I would earn that much on a Saturday, sometimes not. But I would work diligently, until I was way over my income goal. Then I may take a day or two off.

But some days, I …just…didn't…want …to…prospect. I might drive around town, stop for coffee, even go to a movie…Anything to avoid prospecting. And the longer I procrastinated, the more it felt normal….and the harder it was to get back to work.

Somehow, I came up with, what I call "The One Pushup Theory". And it works.

Let's say you want to start an exercise program. And that exercise program starts with pushups.
You work your way up to 100 pushups a day. But today, you just don't feel like doing 100 pushups. What do you do?

Do one pushup. That's right, just do one. Anyone can do a pushup. It takes you no effort at all.

In fact, it's such a small task, you laugh when you consider that you were going to put it off.

So, you get on the floor, get into position, and do that one pushup. Now what?

Well, you're already on the floor. You're already in position, you've already done one pushup…and it didn't kill you. So, you have no reason whatsoever not to do the next one…and the next. And in a few minutes, you cranked out 100 pushups. It's a way to trick your mind, and it works. But it only works, if you are truly willing to stop at one pushup, if you want to. That intention to do just one, has to be real. And momentum carries it through.

I would be driving around town, and think to myself, "OK, I'll knock on just one door, and then go home". Knocking on one door takes no time at all. Blink, and it's over. So, I stop at a house, and knock on that one door, just to get it over with. And you know what? Nobody shot me. Nobody yelled at me. The sky didn't fall. It was effortless. And….since I'm already in the neighborhood, I'm already out of the car, dressed for selling…..I knock on my second door. Now, I'm in the groove, and just keep going.

Make one phone call, knock on one door, visit one business, do one pushup...just one…and let that momentum you just created carry you forward.

I can't count the hundreds of sales I've made, just by making that one prospecting call, which leads to many. This isn't just a theory. It works.

"The grass is always greener on the other side of the fence. Why? Because you aren't looking closely."
— *Claude Whitacre*

Chapter 18

Salary Or Commission - Which Is Better?

Years ago, I had a conversation with a friend who was thinking of getting a job in sales. He asked me which I thought was better, Salary or Commission.

This was my answer.

"Here's what a salary is: an agreement between you and your employer that they will pay you a certain sum per hour. Let's say $10 an hour. Your work will make your employer much more than $10 an hour, or you'll lose your job. So the agreement is; Your employer will pay you the FIRST $10 an hour that you earn for him. *and he keeps the rest.*"

FRIEND: "What do you mean 'The rest'?"

ME: "If you get paid $10 an hour, but you generate *less* than $10 an hour in profits to your employer, how long do you keep your job?"

FRIEND: "Not long, I guess"

ME: "Right, in fact most employers make a *multiple* of your salary off your results They *have* to, if they want the business to grow"

FRIEND: "That almost seems unfair"

ME: "Actually, it's completely fair. If you agree to work for a specific amount & they give it to you, how can it be unfair?"

FRIEND: "So what's so great about commission?"

ME: "This, You know the employer that pays you $10 an hour? *He's* on commission. Every CEO of a company, every self-employed person, every farmer, every landlord, almost *every* wealthy person in the *world* works on the profit of their work, we call it a commission"

FRIEND: "You make commission sound better"

ME: "It *is* better. You ever hear of someone getting promoted to Partner in a business?"

FRIEND: "Sure"

ME: "The person *was* making a salary. When they become a partner, they now get a share of the company's profits; A Commission. Commission is a Promotion. Commission is *more*"

That ended the conversation. It would make a better story if I knew what happened to my friend. I really don't know. We lost touch after that. But years later, when I met my future Brother-in-Law, he asked me where I was employed. I said "I'm not employed" He said "You don't have a job?" Me- "No, I have eight employees. They have jobs. I have a *Company*."

That felt pretty good.

"The longer you stick with a company that keeps its word, the more momentum you build with your customers. Longevity with a company builds trust in the mind of customers."

– Claude Whitacre

Chapter 19

The Single Best Selling Secret To Send Your Sales Through The Roof.

The 5 Lists.

In my long journey, learning to sell at the highest levels, there were discoveries that created giant leaps in my production, and sales numbers. Some of these discoveries would come later in my life, and are pretty advanced.

The discovery I'm going to give you now is one of those. The great news is that this idea can be implemented by someone who is just starting out in their sales careers.
This will work for any product, and company, and any type of selling. My closing rate improved dramatically the week after I did this exercise. I call it "The Five Lists".

This will take a few hours, if done in earnest. You can do this on your computer, but it's better if you write these lists on paper. If you want to transfer the lists online, that's fine. But write them out by hand at first. The memory will be stronger if you write by hand. Although I've always done this on my own, it's a great sales training class to do in a group. What the manager does not want to do, is create the lists and just hand them out. The actual creation of the lists by the new salesperson is the most important part of the process.

Let's get started. Take a sheet of paper, and at the top, write…..

Features of your offer;

Every offer has features. Whether you sell intangibles like life insurance, memberships, seminars, consulting……or sell products you can demonstrate.

Every offer has features. These are the parts of your offer. Take a piece of paper and write down every single feature of your offer. Skip a few lines between features. You should have at least 25 features. When I was selling a vacuum cleaner, I had 117 features listed. When I was selling online marketing services, my list was about 150 features.

One trap, is naming a feature, that is really several features. For example, when I was selling vacuum cleaners, a feature could have been "roller brush for carpet". But it was really;

1) Metal roller brush
2) Replaceable brushes on roller brush
3) Sealed ball bearings on roller
4) Rubber bumpers on end of roller
5) Natural bristle brushes
6) 5 Year warranty on Roller

See? You need to list every single part of every single part. Now, if you sell industrial equipment, you need to list components or assemblies, not every single part. But you should end up with at least 100 features to your offer. If you sell from a catalog of hundreds of items, pick a profitable item that you frequently sell. This exercise will teach you how to *think* about what you sell. Once you do it one time, you'll be able to do it much faster the second time, for a different product. After that, it will be an automatic way of thinking. Anyway, do this list first. Complete it, before you go to the second list. And make three copies of your list of features. It will save some time later.

Benefit of feature to user;

Now, take a copy of your list of features. (Did you remember to leave some space between features?) And then write down, after each feature, the benefit of that feature to the customer. There can be several benefits to one feature. This will be your longest list. These benefits must be something that the customer would agree are to their benefit. Another way to think of a benefit is, "What does the customer get out of that feature?"

And, in my entire life, I haven't seen a feature that didn't have at least one benefit to the buyer.

Take another copy of your list of features.

Competitive features.

Now, beside each feature, write the advantages of each feature over a competitor's features.

If you have a major competitor, compare a feature to what the competition has. How is your feature better?

Language is important here. For example, you sell gym memberships for a year, and your competitor sells them for 3 months at a time.

For example;
"A year membership gives you the time needed to see real benefits" and "A year membership helps insure that you won't quit, before you see the real results you want".

But, what if *you* sell the 3 months memberships? "We don't tie you down to a long term commitment, in case you move or get sick".

Some of these are also benefits of features. But this list is for features that are different than a competitor's.

Not every feature will compare to a competitor's. What I did, is take every feature that is common to most major competitors. At the end of this list, you are nearly done.

Why buy from us?

This is a separate list. This list gives reasons, from the customer's view…that buying from you is a good idea.

This list is different from the "competitive advantages" list. This gives reasons to buy from you, rather than from someone else, selling the exact offer that you sell. This is about your business, and what you offer the customer…as a business…that others don't.
This may be a very short list. You may even just want this to be a list of why they should buy from you personally. My list was why they should buy from me.

This list will focus on what you bring to the table, or what your business brings to the table. This list is answering the question, "Why buy from me, rather than buy the exact same thing from another supplier"

Why buy now?

This last list, gives reasons that it's to the buyer's advantage to buy from you now…as opposed to later.

Examples are;

"Prices will increase"

"The current product will cost more in service, the older it gets"

"The current product will be worth the most as a trade-in, right now"

"These is a sale going on right now"

"They will be the first in their area"

"By buying now, they get an exclusive area"

"They will benefit from this, before their competition does"

You get the idea. You only really need a few good reasons to buy now.

Now, why did I have you create these lists?

First, what have you got in your hands? *Every reason for the prospect to buy what you sell, from you, right now.* You may have a list of 100 real reasons to buy your offer. Maybe even 200.

You have clarified your thinking. Your product knowledge has probably doubled. Your sales ammunition has probably tripled. You now have far more reasons for the prospect to buy than they can ever think of…not to buy.

Second, You now have far better answers to customer questions. When someone asks, "Why do I need this?", you'll have at least one answer that will make sense to them, *and will further the sale*.

The third point is so important, it deserves its own chapter.

Chapter 20

This Technique Will Practically Guarantee A Sale And Keep The Prospect From Shopping.

Third, and this is the most important part…..

When presenting, you need to fit your features and benefits precisely to what your customer wants.

Not every feature will apply to every prospective customer. A major mistake new salespeople make (and some veterans), is that they feel the need to explain every feature that their offer has….even the features that don't apply to the customer.

And, every time you show a feature that the buyer doesn't want...they think "This isn't for me". Have you ever had a presentation that went well, but they didn't buy? This may have been the reason.

These lists give you plenty to talk about, even if only a small number of features apply to the customer's needs. If you have 150 benefits to talk about, and only six benefits are valuable to the customer...you can concentrate on those six benefits, and make the sale based on those benefits alone. That way, in the prospect's mind, your product/service is a perfect fit for them. And you can customize your presentation to fit your offer to them perfectly.

This is assuming that your offer really is to their benefit. And, if you have a better product for them, show it instead. But, in my experience, very few of the features an offer has are really important to the buyer. But you need to know how to talk about those features, no matter what they are.

If you skipped to this part of the chapter without creating your lists...shame on you. You are cheating yourself out of a great way to double your sales. And you can do this exercise right now, before your next appointment.

Chapter 21

Questions You Must Know The Answer To.

Questions new reps should be able to answer.

This section is for both managers and sales reps. If you are the sales manager, each of these questions could be the topic of a sales meeting.

If you are the sales rep, you should ask your manager these questions. This information will fill out a far better understanding of your business, and how to sell.

The Questions

- What are all of the problems we solve?
- How many applications are there for our products/services? What are they?
- How are we better?
- How are we different?
- How do we position ourselves in the marketplace?
- Who are our customers?
- What are their titles?
- How do we get to them?
- Why will they see me?
- What does the first prospecting call sound like? (no matter who makes it)
- What is our sales process?
- How do I navigate the process?
- What are the questions I should be asking the prospect?
- What common objections will I hear?
- How do I handle those objections?
- What does our competition say about us?
- How do we sell against our competitors?
- What are their strengths and weaknesses?
- How do they sell against us?
- How are our prices compared with the competition?
- How do we justify our prices?

Why should you take the time to go over every one of these questions? Because the worst time to need the answer to any one of these questions, is in front of a sales prospect.

The worst time to not have the answer, is during a sales appointment.

"Continue practicing, reading sales books written by successful salespeople. See lots of prospects."
— *Claude Whitacre*

Chapter 22

The Biggest Secret Of The Sales Superstars...... Continuous Learning And Training

You now have the foundation you need to start a career in selling. You have tools to build excellent product knowledge. You have had the beginner mistakes explained so you won't have to experience them as I did.

Combined with your company's training, you have a great start to your sales career.

Now for some bad news… Most salespeople fail. They fail to make a living at selling, and eventually quit the business of selling altogether.

But why is this true?

They stop learning. They stop training. After the new salesperson makes their first sale (even if it's to their Mom) they think "Well, now I know how to do that". Whenever you stop training, and stop learning…that's where your income stops growing. That exact day.

After the initial training given by the company, most salespeople stop learning about how selling works. Can you imagine someone taking a week of engineering school, or three days of medical school, or two weeks of law...and then try to help patients and clients? They would fail. But the average new sales person, once they have taken their company's initial introductory training, effectively stop learning.

"I don't need training". Imagine a surgeon without training. Do you want to be his patient?

I know hundreds of Top Flight salespeople. They come in all ages, sizes, temperament. A few are raging optimists, and few are pessimistic.

But they have two things in common;
1) They work. They put in the effort.
2) They are students of selling. They are constantly improving their technique...their skills.

Personally, I read about a book every few days. These are books on sales, marketing, advertising, how the mind works, and related subjects. I have a library in my home that has over 2,000 books on these subjects.

Do you need to read that many books? Of course not. I buy the books, because I like having them at arm's reach. But you can get them at the library. I have a few books I recommend, at the end of this book. Of course, I include the books I've written.

By continuous training, I mean talking to successful salespeople, watching training videos (many excellent ones are on YouTube.), practicing sales techniques with your fellow salespeople, attending sales meetings, working with several different top salespeople, and of course, reading books by the best salespeople.

In fact, in my sales career, my income has a tendency to grow in huge jumps…then plateau at the new level..then jump again….then level off. Why?

Because huge increases in my income generally came right after I discovered a better way to sell, or a better way to prospect, or a new technique I got from a top salesperson in a different field.

Do you want to know how to never have a sales slump? Keep learning. Every new thing you learn, makes you eager to try it…to see it work. It's impossible to get bored if you are in the process of learning something useful.

And while you are learning, keep working. You learn so much quicker if you can attach what you learn to your daily sales experience. Learning and selling happen side by side.

Continue practicing, reading sales books written by successful salespeople. See lots of prospects.
In a few months, you'll be making a good living. In a year, you'll be great. In 5 years you'll be the best in your company. In ten years you'll be a Legend. Really.

Imagine one day, you are the keynote speaker at your industry's convention. You walk into the room, walking up to the stage….and you hear people whispering, "That's him" and "That's the guy".

It can happen. How do I know?

                        That's what happened to me.

About The Author

Claude Whitacre has been selling to consumers, belly to belly, for 40 years. First, selling life insurance, then vacuum cleaners, then high end online marketing services to local business owners. He now divides his time between speaking to groups of business owners and salespeople about increasing their sales, and selling high end marketing services to business owners. He also owns a retail store in Wooster, Ohio, with his wife Cheryl.

Other Books by Claude Whitacre
- *The Unfair Advantage Small Business Advertising Manual*
- *Selling Local Advertising*
- *Local Online Marketing*
- *One Call Closing*
- *Sales Prospecting*

For information about booking Claude to speak for your group, just go to http://www.ClaudeWhitacre.com/
Or e-mail Claude@LocalProfitGeyser.com

Claude speaks to groups of salespeople and groups of business owners, and nobody else.

A QUICK NOTE FROM CLAUDE...

One Last Thing... If you found this book useful, I'd be very grateful if you'd post a short review on Amazon. Your support really does make a difference and I read all the reviews personally so I can get your feedback and make this book even better. If you'd like to leave a review, all you need to do is find my book on Amazon and leave your review.

Thanks again for your support!

"In a few months, you'll be making a good living.

In a year, you'll be great.

In 5 years you'll be the best in your company.

In ten years you'll be a Legend. Really."

– Claude Whitacre

Recommended Reading

1. **Sales Prospecting:** The Ultimate Guide To Referral Selling, Social Contact Marketing, Telephone Prospecting, And Cold Calling To Find Highly Likely Prospects You Can Close In One Call *by Claude Whitacre*

   If you are a salesperson who is looking for a proven method to multiply your sales prospecting results, you have just found the Motherload. Written by a salesman who practices what he preaches. Every method is field tested and proven. Complete with every script, answers to every objection, and every resource you need to send your sales prospecting results through the roof.

2. **One Call Closing:** The Ultimate Guide To Closing Any Sale In Just One Sales Call *by Claude Whitacre*

   Stop making sales call after sales call, on prospects that are never going to buy from you. Imagine closing 80-90% of your prospects on your first sales appointment, without having to lower your price. This is the insider's guide to closing sales: Finally, get the secrets your sales manager will never tell you and probably doesn't know.

3. **Selling Local Advertising:** The Best Kept Insider Secrets To Create Local Advertising Sales, FAST! *by Claude Whitacre*

    Stop believing the lies and myths that keep you from being the top advertising rep in your city. Stop listening to gurus that never sold anything in their life. Do you sell advertising to local small business owners? Selling Local Advertising is written specifically for advertising sales reps and their managers. Written by someone who sells advertising, but who has bought hundreds of thousands of dollars in local advertising, and has interviewed hundreds of small business owners...your customers.

4. **Local Online Marketing:** Small Business Online Advertising For Retail And Service Businesses *by Claude Whitacre*

    For small business owners who are losing money to online price-slashing competitors! Local Online Marketing was written specifically for the small business owner that has a retail store or service business serving their local area....and nobody else.

5. The Unfair Advantage Small Business Advertising Manual: How to use Newspaper, Direct Mail, Radio, Cable TV, Yellow Pages, and other ... profits in your retail or service business. *by Claude Whitacre*

Inside The Unfair Advantage Small Business Advertising Manual you'll find the following:

- How to know if your advertising is paying off.
- How to avoid all the advertising mistakes that cost you BIG.
- Tips that can double your ad profits.
- How only 2% of our gross sales generates 70% of our profits.
- What advertising methods are a complete waste of money and why.
- The 8 myths that advertising reps tell you.
- The single most profitable part of any ad, that most advertisers completely ignore.
- The most profitable ways to advertise, and why.
- Where you can get Free Advertising for your small business.
- The real secrets of getting wealthy in your own business.

All This And More For The Price Of A Cheap Lunch!

6. **Go Pro:** 7 Steps to Becoming a Network Marketing Professional *by Eric Worre*
7. **Fanatical Prospecting:** The Ultimate Guide for Starting Sales Conversations and Filling the Pipeline by Leveraging Social Selling, Telephone, E-Mail, and Cold Calling *by Jeb Blount*
8. **Pitch Anything:** An Innovative Method for Presenting, Persuading, and Winning the Deal *by Oren Klaff*
9. **The Challenger Sale:** Taking Control of the Customer Conversation *by Matthew Dixon*
10. **Influence:** Science and Practice *by Robert B. Cialdini*
11. **Sell or Be Sold:** How to Get Your Way in Business and in Life *by Grant Cardone*
12. **Go for No!** Yes is the Destination, No is How You Get There *by Richard Fenton*
13. **The Magic of Thinking Big** *by David J. Schwartz*
14. **To Sell Is Human:** The Surprising Truth About Moving Others *by Daniel H. Pink*
15. **Little Red Book of Selling:** 12.5 Principles of Sales Greatness *by Jeffrey Gitomer*
16. **The Go-Giver, Expanded Edition:** A Little Story About a Powerful Business Idea *by Bob Burg*
17. **SPIN Selling:** Situation Problem Implication Need-Payoff *by Neil Rackham*

18. **The SPIN Selling Fieldbook:** Practical Tools, Methods, Exercises, and Resources *by Neil Rackham*
19. **Predictable Prospecting:** How to Radically Increase Your B2B Sales Pipeline *by Marylou Tyler*
20. **Fanatical Prospecting:** The Ultimate Guide for Starting Sales Conversations and Filling the Pipeline by Leveraging Social Selling, Telephone, E-Mail, and Cold Calling *by Jeb Blount*
21. **How I Raised Myself from Failure to Success in Selling** *by Frank Bettger*
22. **If You're Not First, You're Last:** Sales Strategies to Dominate Your Market and Beat Your Competition *by Grant Cardone*
23. **The 10X Rule:** The Only Difference Between Success and Failure *by Matthew Dixon & Brent Adamson*
24. **The Prosperous Coach:** Increase Income and Impact for You and Your Clients *by Steve Chandler*
25. **The Secrets of Closing the Sale** *by Zig Ziglar*

www.ingramcontent.com/pod-product-compliance
Lightning Source LLC
Chambersburg PA
CBHW071818200526
45169CB00018B/418